D1083579

Indian Nations

THE SHOSHONE

by
Ned Blackhawk

General Editors
Herman J. Viola and David Jeffery

A Rivilo Book

RAINTREE
STECK-VAUGHN
PUBLISHERS

A Harcourt Company

Austin • New York
www.steck-vaughn.com

Published by Raintree Steck-Vaughn Publishers, an imprint of the Steck-Vaughn Company

Developed for Steck-Vaughn Company by Rivilo Books

Editor: David Stern	Raintree Steck-Vaughn Publishers Staff
Photo Research: Paula Dailey	Publishing Director: Walter Kossmann
Design: Barbara Lisenby and Todd Hirshman	Editor: Kathy DeVico
Electronic Preparation: Lyda Guz	Electronic Production: Scott Melcer

Photo Credits: Associated Press/AP Photo/Dennis Cook: cover foreground, p. 13; Herman Viola: cover background; Kim Fujiwara: pp. 4, 6; Bruce Dale/National Geographic Image Collection, p. 7; ©Ted Wood: pp. 9 left, 9 bottom right, 11, 22, 23, 24, 25, 39 right; James Amos/National Geographic Image Collection: pp. 12 top, 16 and 17 (prints by William Henry Jackson), 29, 38 top, 38 bottom; Department of Anthropology Research Museum, University of Nevada, Reno: pp. 8, 19 top left, 19 center, p. 19 right (rabbit blanket made by Alice Hooper of Austin, Nevada, circa 1925), p. 20 top; Raquel Chopa/The National Museum of the American Indian Research Branch, New York: p. 9 top; Special Collections Department, University Library, University of Nevada, Reno: pp. 10, 21 all, 27; Ned Blackhawk: pp. 15 (pictured in photo Jessie, Angline, Emma Dyer, Annie Snooks), 30, 36 top, 36 bottom, 39 left, 40, 41; Smithsonian Anthropological Archives (SAA): p. 12 bottom; William H. Jackson, (SAA): pp. 18, 19, 26, 31, 32; Baker and Johnston (SAA), Original print donated by Mrs. Alice N. Hunt: p. 12; School of American Research, Santa Fe: p. 20 all; Museum of New Mexico: p. 29 bottom; ©Will Powers: p. 33; ©Ilka Hartmann: p. 37; Katrina Lasko: p. 46.

Acknowledgments: The author thanks the various museums for their time and assistance: the Peabody Museum, Harvard University; the National Museum of the American Indian Research Branch, New York; the School of American Research, Santa Fe; the Museum of New Mexico, Santa Fe; the University of Nevada, Reno's Anthropology Department and Special Collections; and the Hearst Museum, University of California, Berkeley. Raquel Chopa at the NMAI provided invaluable assistance and support throughout. Special thanks to Catherine Fowler, Darla Gregg, and other staff members at UNR.

Library of Congress Cataloging-in-Publication-Data

Blackhawk, Ned.
      The Shoshone/by Ned Blackhawk.
         p.   cm. — (Indian nations)
      Includes bibliographical references and index.
      Summary: Introduces the history, culture, and daily life of the Shoshone Indians and examines the challenges they have faced since their first contact with Europeans.
      ISBN 0-8172-5468-4
      1. Shoshoni Indians — Juvenile literature. [1. Shoshoni Indians.
2. Indians of North America.] I. Title. II. Series: Indian nations
(Austin, Tex.)
E99.S4B53   2000
~~978.004 9745 — DC21~~   99-23347
                                CIP

Printed and bound in the United States of America
1 2 3 4 5 6 7 8 9 0 LB 03 02 01 00

Cover photo: Randy 'L He-dow Teton (Shoshone-Bannock) from Lincoln Creek district of Fort Hall, Idaho. Her name means "meadowlark" or "close to ground." She modeled for the Sacagawea dollar coin. The background shows the Grand Tetons in Wyoming.

Contents

Cottontail Shoots at the Sun

One day long ago, when animals talked and were related to humans, Cottontail was hot and angry. It had been a very long and hot summer. Up above Sun burned down. Sun turned plants brown, dried the riverbeds, and almost dried the springs of water that everyone needed to survive. Some water still ran but only in small, shaded canyons. Cottontail was tired of the dryness that was turning his beautiful coat dull and lifeless. He told everyone that he was going to shoot Sun. "When Sun comes," Cottontail said, "I will shoot him and end this hot dryness."

So Cottontail made a bow and some arrows. He chipped flint for arrowheads, and he sharpened the flint with deer horn. He baked the points with poison. Then he started making a bow, and he made a bow string of sinew (animal tendon). He used feathers from Gopher Hawk for his arrows. Then he went to find Sun.

Sun is vulnerable when he first peeps over the horizon to see who may be lurking about. Sun tricked Cottontail by coming out in different places every day, farther and farther to the north. Finally, Cottontail judged where Sun would come out next. When Sun peered over the horizon at dawn, Cottontail jumped up from hiding and began shooting. Cottontail's arrows went straight but burned in Sun's heat. Cottontail put his bow down and picked up a stone. He threw the stone and hurt Sun.

◀ *Cottontail shoots at the Sun in a Shoshone folktale.*

Sun became very angry and poured hot fire all over Earth. Cottontail ran and ran but had no place to hide. "Run away," said Deer. "Fly away," said the Birds. "Keep running," said the Trees. Finally, Cottontail asked Bush if he could hide him. "Just my top burns; my roots don't burn," said Bush. So Cottontail dug a hole under Bush and hid in it. After a while, Cottontail wondered if the fire was gone, so he looked out from his hiding place. But it was too soon. The top of his head and back were burned a deep brown, the color they are today—a reminder to everyone of his foolish challenge to mighty Sun.

Creation Story

The many stories and myths of the Shoshone, or **Newe**, as they call themselves, are similar yet somewhat different for every Shoshone tribe. The stories are handed down from generation to generation. In the old days, everyone gathered around fires at night to hear the storytellers describe how long, long ago animals and people were very much alike. Stories like the one about Cottontail shooting at Sun entertained youngsters and helped teach them how to respect nature and their elders. These lessons, taught over and over, were a part of a child's earliest memories, and children often fell asleep listening to them.

One story tells how the Shoshone became the children of Coyote. A long time ago, Coyote lived by himself. One day, he was busy making a rabbit snare when a beautiful but strange young woman peeked inside his home. She didn't say a word and left right away. Coyote thought she was beautiful, so he followed her. He couldn't see her, but he followed her tracks. Finally, when they came to a river, Coyote found the girl. "Get on my back," she told him, "and I will take you across the river." Coyote climbed on her back, and they went across the river.

Shoshone stories give great power to Coyote and other "Trickster" figures.

7

The girl took Coyote to her mother's home. He spent several days and nights in their home, helping with chores. One morning when they awoke, the girl gave birth to many, many little people. The mother told Coyote to go fetch some water, but the jug she gave him was made like a basket and leaked. Down at the river, Coyote had to soak the jug until it swelled up enough to stop the leaks.

When Coyote returned, the mother and daughter were gone, and they had taken many of the little people with them far to the East. Coyote put those remaining, the Newe, into his jug and started for home. Soon he heard a lot of noise coming from the jug—laughing, hollering, and other mischief-making. He was tired of carrying the jug, so he set it down and opened it. All of a sudden, many of the little people ran away. They ran south. The rest stayed in the jug, and Coyote brought them home, washed, and cleaned them. Then he let them go. This is how all the people were created.

Some baskets were so tightly woven that they could carry water.

Prehistory and Geography

According to their stories, Shoshone peoples have lived in their homelands in the **Great Basin** since the beginning of time. Little is known about people from times so long ago. Some relics, such as fossilized food remains and tools, have been found, but very little is known about their important ways and beliefs. Petroglyphs, or paintings on rock, have been found in Nevada, Wyoming, and Idaho, where Shoshone peoples once lived, but it is hard to say what they mean.

Made of all natural materials, this duck decoy (above) is one of the earliest known cultural artifacts of the Great Basin peoples. Petroglyphs (left and below), look scary, but are representations of animals, plants, and human beings.

The different Shoshone peoples in this large area did not call themselves "Shoshone." The origins of that word are unclear. Most likely it was used by Europeans who were confused about names. The Shoshone all considered themselves to be Newe and spoke versions of the Shoshone language called **Numic**.

Like Cottontail, the Shoshone people lived in a world that could be very hot and dry. Finding good food and clean water was essential. Hunting such animals as deer, antelope, rabbits, and even small field mice provided meat, but Shoshones fed

themselves mainly by gathering plants. The delicious and nutritious nuts of the **piñon** (pine tree) was their main food. In the fall, Shoshones came together to harvest these valuable nuts, and during the winter they lived off their stored harvest. In the spring and summer, they moved through their country in small numbers to harvest seeds and grasses and to hunt the many different animals. Telling stories around the winter fires and gathering for big events in the harvest months were the main social activities of the people for a very long time.

About 1,000 years ago, Numic-speaking peoples moved southward out of the Great Basin. Like the little people in Coyote's water jug, people in modern Arizona and Mexico speak languages related to Numic. Among them are the Indians of Mexico who still speak Aztec and the Hopi Indians of Arizona. About 500 years ago, other Shoshone peoples also moved north into the mountain regions of Wyoming and Idaho and began to adopt the ways of their neighbors. Now there are many different Shoshone-speaking people and different Shoshone tribes.

Piñon pine cones contain seeds, or nuts, which make nutritious food.

The almost three million acres of the desert-like Wind River Reservation in Wyoming is shared by the Eastern Shoshone and Northern Arapaho peoples.

Geography

The homeland in the Great Basin of the U.S. West is called **Newe Sogobia** in Shoshone. Although American explorer John Frémont gave the Great Basin its name, it is not one big basin but hundreds of smaller basins with many mountain ridges and valley floors. Different Shoshone peoples have lived in small bands in these valleys and mountains and consider them their homelands. They lived as far south as Death Valley, California, and as far north as Yellowstone National Park (Wyoming, Idaho, southern Montana). Much of the basin receives very little rain, and water is often hard to find. Although it looks like a desert with sagebrush, sandy dirt, and flats with alkaline soil that tastes bitter, Shoshones consider this earth to be beautiful and thank it for all its gifts. To the north, Shoshone peoples were fortunate to fish along the Snake and other rivers or live in mountains more than 10,000 feet (3,050 m) high. The different terrain and climates of those regions influenced Shoshone peoples' lives. It determined what animals they could hunt or fish, and what plants they could gather to cook and eat.

Key Historical Events

Beginning in the early 1600s, European contacts began to change the lives of the Shoshone. The first wild horses in North America came from herds brought by Spanish colonists. Shoshone peoples on the Great Plains traded for horses with their Indian neighbors. Other European items came into Shoshone hands. Metal tools and glass beads helped them in their daily lives. But diseases and alcohol brought by the Europeans destroyed thousands of Shoshone people.

Since the other tribes around them also used the horse, the Northern Shoshone competed for precious resources. To get

Horses, such as these sketched on a cliff wall (above), were descended from animals that escaped from Spanish herds. Later, the Spanish and Shoshone opened direct trade. The Indians especially liked attractive objects that could be worn on clothes, like the brass studs, beads, and mirror on this warrior (left) in about 1890.

12

firearms, horses, and control of buffalo herds, tribes on the plains often raided and fought one another.

By the mid-1700s, Spaniards began to establish settlements in California, and traders and explorers began to explore the lands between Spanish outposts. The Old Spanish Trail between Santa Fe and Los Angeles passed directly through Shoshone homelands in Utah, Nevada, and California. Shoshones faced new pressures, particularly the Spanish demand for food sources, water supplies, and Indian slaves. These first encounters taught the Shoshone that European newcomers brought dramatic and deadly changes with them.

In the early 1800s, both Great Britain and the United States competed for control of the western half of North America. British and then American traders moved rapidly into the Great Basin along the Snake and Humboldt rivers. With the aid of local Shoshone guides, Americans explored and hunted animals. Sacagawea, a young Shoshone girl, helped American explorers Meriwether Lewis and William Clark scout the enormous Louisiana Purchase and find their way to the Pacific Ocean. She interpreted Indian languages for them and even helped them find food.

Later in the 1800s, the Western Shoshone of Nevada, California, and Utah, and the Northern Shoshone

First Lady Hillary Rodham Clinton admires the design of a new dollar coin honoring Sacagawea, who helped Lewis and Clark. With her is Randy 'L He-dow Teton, who modeled for the coin, which was designed by Glenna Goodacre.

of Wyoming and Idaho all faced European newcomers. Some smaller Shoshone groups joined together under powerful leaders, while others migrated out of disease-infested areas and into remote mountain locations.

The United States conquered northern Mexico in the Mexican-American War of 1846–1848, and the United States gained control of the Southwest and California. The **California Gold Rush** attracted more than 100,000 miners and settlers out West in the 1840s and 1850s. Tens of thousands of those pioneers passed directly through the Great Basin, damaging the fragile habitat with their many horses and cattle. They often attacked whatever small bands of Shoshones they encountered. At Bear River in Idaho, a group of American volunteer soldiers massacred nearly 300 Shoshone, mostly women and children. Thousands of Shoshones, especially around mining settlements, did not survive those violent years of foreign invasion.

Throughout the 1800s, Indian peoples in the Great Basin continued to witness American aggression. Eastern California and Nevada were abundant in timber and mineral resources, which the Americans took. The U.S. government negotiated **treaties** in the mid-1800s with most Shoshone groups outside of California. The treaties were supposed to protect certain Shoshone lands to be set aside as reservations. The treaties were also supposed to pay Shoshone peoples for the lands and resources the government took from them. The Shoshone did not receive the reservations and payments that were agreed to. Over and over again, the government broke its promises. With their food resources damaged and their lands occupied, the Shoshone faced many hardships. They were given the worst jobs because of the racism of the time. They had to work on white-owned ranches, in mines, or as servants in white households.

Conditions became even harder in the late 1800s and early 1900s, when the U.S. government began new policies that tried to make the Shoshone more like the white man. The government required Shoshone children to attend **boarding schools**, usually far away from their families. In those schools, Shoshone children were forbidden to speak their native language and were beaten if they did. They were forced to cut their hair short, and their old handmade clothes were burned. For many, school was more like a prison, and many Shoshone children ran away.

Their hair cut short in 1926, four girls attended the Reese River Ranch School in Nevada. They lived with their relatives who did ranch work for low wages.

During this period, new laws were passed dealing with Indian people and Indian lands. The **Dawes Act of 1887** and other laws attacked the idea that Indians should own their lands together as a tribe. It gave reservation lands to individual Indians. The results of this and other laws were disastrous for

Indian peoples. Although the Shoshone held onto more land than many of their neighbors, they continued to fight to live on lands they once controlled.

The 1800s and early 1900s were a very difficult time for the Shoshone. Their sufferings, however, were only one side of the story. In the face of such hardships, Shoshone peoples fought back. Great military and political leaders arose, such as Te Moak of the Western Shoshone and Washakie of the Northern Shoshone. Mothers taught their children Shoshone language and culture when they returned from boarding schools. Families moved to new regions to harvest pine nuts, and slowly Shoshone people began to learn the white man's law and language to try to hold the government to its treaties.

The Shoshone suffered, but they also survived. The Shoshone's struggles and survival are what makes them who they are today.

Washakie, a great chief of the Eastern Shoshone, was a scout for the U.S. Army but was furious at the treatment of his people. "The white man kills our game, captures our furs... [The government] does not protect our rights. It leaves us without...seed, without tools...without breeding animals...without the food we still lack...without the schools we so much need for our children."

Way of Life

Shoshone peoples usually lived in small **bands** for most of the year. Every member of each band had specific jobs to do. The children gathered wood and water. Women prepared and cooked the food. Men and teenage boys helped make and repair tools, clothing, and weapons. The work did not take up all of the daylight hours, however. There was still time for recreation, art and games, and sports.

Houses

Before Europeans came, most Shoshone to the south, including the Panamint, Timbisha, and Gosiute Shoshone, lived in small houses of tree branches and willow shoots. To make houses, they cut saplings and fastened them together tightly with strings of animal hide or with twine made out of grasses. They arranged these **wickiups** together in camps and made special

Wickiups were made from young trees that were tightly bound together and sometimes covered with grass mats. Another, heavier type of wickiup was made from branches that supported hides or canvas (left).

The Northern and Eastern Shoshone eventually adopted the housing style of the Plains Indians. This 1878 tipi resembles those of the Lakota Sioux.

houses for social and ceremonial occasions. Girls, for instance, had their own houses when they first entered womanhood. Southern Shoshones moved often, and the wickiups were easy to pack up and carry.

In the mountain areas of Wyoming, Idaho, and Montana, Shoshones lived in lodges covered with elk and buffalo hides. After the arrival of the horse, these Northern and Eastern Shoshone adopted many of the ways of their Indian neighbors on the Great Plains. They hunted buffalo, raided other tribes on horseback, and traded with other tribes as well as with Europeans.

Clothes

In the colder climates and higher elevations of the Great Basin, Shoshone peoples wore close-fitting buckskins made mostly from deer and elk hides. In the warmer regions, men wore short pants and sandals, while women wore woven mats and woven hats to protect themselves from the Sun.

At night, when it sometimes dropped below freezing and snowed, Shoshones tucked under their beloved rabbit blankets. Each blanket was made of dozens of individual rabbit skins. Rabbits were skinned so that the fur was in one long piece. Dozens of the long pieces were sewn together to make a very warm and comfortable blanket.

A vest and moccasins (above) show expert beadwork. Blankets made of rabbit pelts (right) eased the chill of winter. By the early 1900s, clothing made of cloth was in widespread use, as in the robes of a woman named Jenny Washington (below).

After they adopted the horse, Northern and Eastern Shoshone people began to wear clothing similar to that of their neighbors, particularly buffalo robes and buckskin garments. The Western Shoshone adopted many of the styles of European and American newcomers. They took the nice cotton and wool American fabrics and made long and comfortable clothing. Since many of today's Shoshone work on ranches, they wear the classic western-style clothing: big hats, boots, and fancy western shirts and dresses. They often make the clothes look fancier with embroidered designs and beaded items, such as big belt buckles.

Arts and Crafts

For the Shoshone, art serves many purposes. While crafts have specific functions in daily life, they also express Shoshone values, beliefs, and skills. Western Shoshone baskets, for example, were beautiful artistic creations that were so tightly woven they held water and were used to cook and store food. Shoshone women often wove animal figures and other symbols in the design of their baskets. The symbols told where the basket maker came from or what spirits helped the maker create the basket. Basketmaking was one of the most developed artistic traditions of the Shoshone, and Shoshone baskets are considered some of the finest in the world.

An especially fine basket was made with a lizard design.

With their close ties to the plains, the Northern and Eastern Shoshone adopted traditions and practices of their neighbors. For example, using large buffalo or elk hides, they made **hide paintings** to record the great events in their history. They used beads, elk teeth, animal claws, and porcupine quills to decorate moccasins, dresses, and other items of clothing. Beading, basketmaking, and hide paintings are just a few of the many beautiful and complex Shoshone artistic traditions.

Painted on elk hide, this late 19th century scene features the sacred Sun Dance in the middle. It is surrounded by buffalo, or bison, and galloping horsemen.

Food

The Western Shoshone hunted deer, antelope, rabbits, and a variety of small game. The Northern and Eastern Shoshone hunted much larger elk, buffalo, and bighorn sheep. They also fished much more than the Western Shoshone. As had been true in the distant past, the gathering of local plants was an important source of food. Shoshones have harvested piñon pine nuts in the autumn since the beginning of time and have prepared them in many different ways. When ground up, pine nuts form a paste that can be rolled into bread dough. Nuts can be boiled to make soup. Roasted, they remain good for many months. Shoshone groups saved much of their supply in underground storage pits to eat during the cold winter months. The pine nut plays a significant cultural role and appears in many Great Basin stories and legends.

Pine nuts are removed from the parts of the cone that cannot be eaten. Baskets made of twine (right) are shaken (below) to separate out the nuts.

European contact changed drastically the Shoshones' food sources. For the Northern Shoshone, who hunted on the plains, the near killing off of the buffalo in the late 1800s forever changed their lives. Despite such losses, they have continued to hunt elk, deer, and other animals as they have for countless generations. Shoshone meat stews and fry bread are now often served at family as well as communal gatherings.

American pioneers and miners often destroyed the grasses and pine trees upon which the Western Shoshone depended. Mining in Nevada and eastern California used up much of the local timber and water resources, removing pine trees and drying up many springs. Ranching and pioneer travel through the region destroyed marshes and grasslands along major rivers. Cattle, horses, and sheep ate grasses and seeds that Shoshone women gathered for baskets and foods. As a result, the Shoshone came to depend on local white communities and on the federal government for their survival. The government has given them food and other help. However, poverty and economic problems continue to plague many communities.

Horses graze happily on grassland of the Wind River Reservation. In the 19th century, much of the Shoshone grazing land was damaged by white settlers who put too many animals on the range.

Spiritual Life

The Sun Dance

A long time ago, a man was riding alone in the prairie. As he rode past a buffalo skull, he heard singing. He stopped his horse and got off. The singing was coming from the white buffalo skull. He got down on his knees and looked through the empty eye sockets into the skull. Inside, he saw Indians performing the Sun Dance. The Indians told him of the Sun Dance and the Dance of Thirst and Fasting. They told him he must go without food and water for 3 days and nights until he had a vision. That vision would reveal all the sacred rituals and ceremonies of the Sun Dance.

The Sun Dance still requires great strength, commitment, and preparation. During the ceremony, participants dance and pray for the earth to be as clean and free from disease as the air above. Many songs and rituals must be performed for the ceremony to be right and true.

Shoshone Spirituality

Many Shoshone peoples believe that they live in a highly spiritual world where humans are simply one part of a greater universe. Therefore, animals, the dead, mountains, rivers, and the land itself all have spiritual significance. This is why the Shoshone people thank the spirits of

This man has placed a buffalo skull by the entrance of his sweat lodge for protection. A sweat lodge is like a sweat bath that cleanses a person both physically and spiritually.

23

Washakie Reservoir, in Wyoming. The beautiful land, mountains, and all living beings together have spiritual significance to the Shoshone.

their ancestors and also thank animals for providing food and furs. When an animal is killed in a hunt, for example, a special offering is made to thank the animal's spirit so that it will not be offended. To honor the earth, animals, and ancestors is very important. This is why ancient burial sites are maintained and never uncovered. The Sun Dance is one religious practice that honors and protects the land. But the Shoshone practice many other religions as well.

Different Christian faiths, such as the Church of Latter-Day Saints, or Mormon religion, have followings among today's Shoshone people. However, practicing a Christian religion does

Symbols of Indian spirituality and Catholic Christianity come together in harmony in a church on a reservation.

not mean that people ignore ancestral teachings and practices. Gaining spiritual strength from outside religions and using it for everyday guidance are important as Shoshone communities and cultures continue to change.

Besides adopting Christianity from Europeans and Americans, many Shoshone have learned religious practices from other American Indians. At the end of the 1800s, the Ghost Dance religious movement spread among the Shoshone from their Paiute neighbors. They believed that by performing certain dances and singing certain songs—and by purifying themselves—that the good times they knew before the Europeans came would return again.

After the Ghost Dance movement passed into history, many Shoshone became members of the Native American Church. Using sacred plants and medicines, members fast and pray all night in order to cleanse themselves. A minister, or spiritual leader, guides their service, which involves singing religious songs and administering proper medicines. The Native American Church, like the Sun Dance, is one of many forms of Shoshone religion. Shoshone today follow the teachings of different religions, because all religions give spiritual guidance to live a good life in this world.

Family Life

Before Europeans arrived, Shoshone groups lived most of the year in small family bands. These bands included one set of parents, their children, and sometimes their children's husbands and wives. Elderly aunts, cousins, and grandparents often lived in such family groups when they could no longer lead bands of their own.

Role of Parents

The father was the main leader of the family band. His authority to decide when and where to travel was usually respected by other members. For the Western Shoshone, the father's lineage and rights to the land were the basis for his authority and decision-making powers. When a young woman or man was ready to leave a family unit, for instance, the woman usually traveled to live with her husband's family. At some point, the young couple was ready to set off on their own. Then they would hunt and gather foods in certain locations approved in advance by the husband's father and family.

While lineage and hunting lands usually were traced on the father's side, Shoshone women and mothers were the mainstay of the families. When men were away hunting,

Generations of mothers with a baby tucked into a cradleboard show the strength of family life in 1878.

26

women raised and nurtured the children. When a pregnant woman was about to give birth, the other women in the family, as well as other women from neighboring bands, would come together to help the expectant mother. The women made a special house similar to the wickiup where the baby would come into the world. They helped prepare the birth bed and gathered water and medicines. When the time came, they guided the mother through the birth and welcomed the baby into the world. Women were considered to be close to the powers of ancestors and had to be respected in many ways.

Role of Relatives

Shoshone relatives have long been closely involved in the lives of their extended families. Grandmothers and grandfathers often instructed young ones in the proper ways that humans should live. Shoshone grandparents were expert storytellers. They usually led the family's entertainment at night during the long winter months. Their knowledge and wisdom were very powerful, and all Shoshone peoples respected their older relatives greatly. In more recent times, Shoshone elders have been the ones to remember the older ways and language. They remain figures of great knowledge and respect.

The woven designs on this cradleboard have special significance for the child's family.

Role of Children

As soon as the baby was born, the infant spent special time alone with the mother. She had prepared a special **cradleboard** for her baby. It was made from woven branches and leather. The new mother wove into the cover, or hood, of the cradleboard a beautiful design that identified the baby as a boy or a girl. The mother was always nearby and often carried the cradleboard on her

*A mother and her child went everywhere
together, even as the woman worked.*

back while she worked gathering grasses or performing other chores. The baby was comforted
by his or her mother's voice and the many sweet
songs that only women knew.

When little boys could walk and help out,
they would often accompany their fathers on
hunts or while collecting water and wood. Before
horses and guns were introduced by Europeans,
hunting was more difficult and required greater
strategy and teamwork. The fast deer, for instance,
often escaped Shoshone hunters. Young Shoshone
men, and even boys, helped their fathers and uncles
catch the speedy deer. Spreading themselves out
over a very large area, usually in the mountains where
the deer lived, Shoshone men waited for a deer to come.
When someone spotted one, he would run after it and
try to chase it toward another person. This person
would chase it toward yet another person. This relay race would
continue for many miles, until finally the deer grew tired, and
one of the men could kill it. To hunt deer this way required
strength and endurance. It also required spiritual power, which
Shoshone men greatly respected. A young man or boy who
successfully hunted his first deer, antelope, elk, or bear earned
great respect for his manliness and power. Such men, mothers
told their daughters, made strong and capable husbands.

Young girls usually stayed close to their mother and sisters
and learned about the woman's world. Older girls often spent
much of their youth helping take care of their little brothers
and sisters, changing their dirty clothes and keeping them out

*A girl of about three joins in with her elders at a **powwow**.*

of trouble. They also learned how to cook and prepare special foods. They learned exactly how to gather the right grasses and willows and at what times of year. This was important knowledge for girls to learn so that they could make the baskets, clothes, and tools that their own families would need when they were older.

Games

Living in their cradleboards, Shoshone babies often played with beads and other items dangling down from the hood. Older children had handmade dolls decorated with animal and sometimes human hair to make them more lifelike. Children also played games involving pretend buffalo hunts or other Shoshone activities.

This Indian rag doll from the early 1900s has glass beads on its face.

"Fandango" dancing in Nevada, in the 1920s. As a child, the author attended many group celebrations and festivals, which always included games, socializing, and dances. They remain to him "fondly remembered moments of cultural celebration and pride."

When families gathered together for festivals, children enjoyed all kinds of activities, such as running, dancing, and singing. The most exciting game in Shoshone life has been the hand-and-stick games played mostly by adults. In these games, two sides sit opposite each other. One team has a set of small bones that they pass among themselves. The other team tries to guess which member of the opposite team has the bones. If correct, then they get a stick from the other team. If they are wrong, then they have to give away one of their sticks. When one team is out of sticks, it loses. A team's outcome isn't based on skill alone but also involves spiritual power, or "medicine." Teams sing during the games to invoke the power of their medicine. They believe that when your medicine is strong, you will win.

Tribal Government

Political Leadership and Organization

The many Shoshone tribes have had different forms of leadership and organization. The Western Shoshone of Nevada, California, and Utah lived in small family bands. The Shoshone tribes to the north in Idaho and Wyoming lived in larger groups. Many of those groups migrated onto the plains in search of buffalo. The small bands of the Western Shoshone lived for most of the year in fertile mountain valleys. They all considered themselves part of the people, or Newe. Each band, however, identified itself as unique and separate from other bands. Shoshones usually referred to themselves in terms of the area they lived in or the type of foods that they ate. For instance, in central Nevada a group of Western Shoshone called themselves "deerberry eaters," after the fruit they ate. In other words, the Western Shoshone were not one group but dozens of smaller bands that lived separately in different areas. They were related in terms of language and culture, but they did not all follow one overall leader's authority. Each band usually followed the authority of the father of one family.

Chief Washakie (standing in center front) and other important tribal leaders gather in the Wind River Mountains in 1870.

The Northern and Eastern Shoshone usually lived in much larger groups, not as one or two big tribes but as dozens of tribes. Each lived according to its own beliefs and practices. Tribes often traveled in large groups of many families with centralized leadership and organization. The power to speak for the tribe and to make important decisions, such as when to attack an enemy, generally rested with a war chief. The chief usually gained authority through his deeds in war and hunting. With powerful enemies around them, such as the Blackfeet and the Arapaho, Northern and Eastern Shoshone developed warrior societies. For instance, the practice of **counting coup** was common among the plains Shoshone and their enemies. The French word *coup* means "blow," as in hit or strike. A warrior would attack an enemy both physically and spiritually. Instead of trying to kill an enemy, the warrior would simply strike him

with a "coup stick." This was often a short piece of wood decorated with beads and eagle feathers. The act of counting coup made the enemy feel ashamed, while the Shoshone warrior felt proud to look brave and superior in the eyes of his people.

Leadership was not passed down from fathers to sons but from one brave warrior to another. A chief's eagle feather headdress was often the most visible symbol of authority, and elders in the tribe prepared it in ceremonies with special songs.

Chief Washakie's eagle-feather headdress was a symbol of his standing and authority.

Cultural Leadership and Organization

Among the Northern and Eastern Shoshone, special groups called societies took on responsibilities vital for the day-to-day activities of the tribe. When traveling in large groups, for instance, certain societies of the tribe were responsible for leading the group, while other societies were responsible for making sure that the end of the group kept up with the leaders. That way everyone traveled together, and no one fell too far behind. In the Green River region of Wyoming, for example, Shoshone societies included a group known as the Logs. They were responsible for directing families into the camps, telling them where to set up their lodges, and other tasks. Usually, though, most people knew their responsibilities within the tribes and respected and obeyed their leaders.

All Shoshones also had special religious leaders with great spiritual powers. They often communicated with the spirits of the ancestors, so they held tremendous authority in the tribes. Often seeing both good and bad fortunes in their dreams, the spiritual leaders helped counsel tribal leaders and family members. They helped educate children and young adults about the powers of the world. Their roles in honoring and respecting the spirits of the ancestors, animals, and land required long training and guidance.

Spiritual leader Corbin Harney calls for a return to the "Native way" to heal "Mother Earth."

Contemporary Life

Twentieth Century History

The beginning of the 20th century was a very difficult time for Shoshone peoples. Following decades of population decline and the conquest of their ancestral lands by American invaders, the Shoshone started the 1900s burdened with many pressures.

During the late 1800s, reservations were established for the Shoshone. The Wind River Reservation of Wyoming and Fort Hall Indian Reservation of Idaho were located in the ancestral lands of the Eastern and Northern Shoshone. Although the

Once the Shoshone roamed over a huge area of the American Far West. Today they occupy only several small reservations in Idaho, Nevada, and Wyoming.

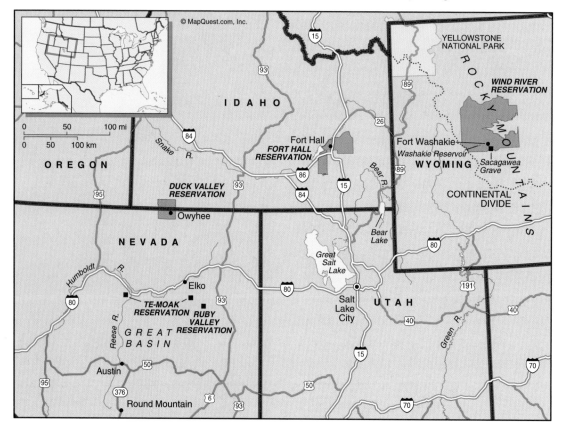

Western Shoshones had lived in a much larger area than the other Shoshones, they were granted only a small reservation at Duck Valley on the Nevada-Idaho border. The U.S. government had agreed in the Treaty of Ruby Valley of 1863 to create reservations for the many Western Shoshone peoples but never lived up to its legal promises. So in the early 1900s, many Shoshone lacked protected lands for hunting and food gathering and had to work for white communities instead.

The 1930s brought changes in Indian policy that ended many of the government's attempts to force Indians into American cultural and economic programs. The land policies of the late 1800s, which had reduced the size of Indian reservations, were changed. Also Indian tribal governments received some power over their own lands and communities.

This **Indian New Deal** also led to the recognition of many new Indian governments as well as the creation of new Indian reservations, including several small reservations for the Western Shoshone. Unfortunately for many Indian peoples, this era of limited self-rule was quickly followed in the 1950s by another attempt to end the unique legal status of Indian tribes. This new policy was called **Termination**, and it took away federal resources and protection for Indian peoples. Fortunately, though, the Shoshone did not lose their limited power of self-government.

In addition, the U.S. government tried to bring Indians into the larger U.S. society through **Relocation** programs. These moved Indian peoples away from their reservations to work in cities. Only in the 1970s did these programs give way to an era of **Indian Self-Determination**, in which Indian peoples and tribal governments helped determine and enforce the laws under which they would live.

Contemporary Communities

Since World War II, Shoshones have experienced lots of changes. For many Shoshone men, the war was the first time that they had ever left their homelands and country. Like their brave fathers, grandfathers, and uncles, Shoshone men served their people proudly during the war.

After the war, partly due to the relocation programs of the government, many young Shoshones began to move farther and farther away

Veteran Cleveland Mike fought for his country in Korea.

from their reservations. Many Western Shoshone who did not have reservations started living in Indian communities in the cities of Nevada. These communities are called **colonies** and, with federal funding and local tribal governments, now have a status similar to Indian reservations. Besides these colonies, numerous Shoshones moved to larger cities looking for work.

Moving to cities changed the lives of Shoshone families both on and off the reservations. Children learned to speak English and were taught American values in cities and schools far away from reservations, but they still kept Shoshone identities and culture.

When the Charley family of Austin, Nevada, posed for a portrait, Marvin, Beverly, and Versa put on their best faces. Evan, in the back, couldn't resist the chance to play the clown. He is now the author's father.

In the past few decades, Shoshone reservations have gained increasing control over their own communities and resources, with their own schools, health services, courts, and police forces.

One of the main battles recently for the Shoshone has been the land claims struggle in Nevada. Western Shoshone tribes want the government to give back much of the land it stole in the 19th century. The government has offered to pay millions of dollars for the land it took, but many Shoshone want their ancestral homelands returned to their control.

Sisters Mary (left) and Carrie (right) Dann fought legal battles against the U.S. Bureau of Land Management for years over ranching rights in eastern Nevada.

Contemporary Culture

Shoshone Indians continue many of the beliefs and practices that they have had since the beginning of time. People still harvest pine nuts in the fall to thank their ancestors and the Earth for lasting nourishment. The Sun Dance and the Native American Church also continue on reservation communities, as do many Christian denominations.

All finery on display, a young man (above) joins in the celebrations at a powwow on the Shoshone-Bannock Reservation. Hearts pound during a mounted relay race (left) at the Eastern Idaho State Fair, in Blackfoot, Idaho.

Shoshones have also adopted many exciting activities from other Indians as well as from Americans. Powwows, especially in the summer, attract Shoshone and other Indians from all over. Rodeos and other western attractions are also very popular. Shoshones have for generations been some of the best cowboys, or buckaroos, in the West.

Although pressures from Europeans and then Americans have altered the quality of life for the Shoshone, they continue to live according to their own beliefs and traditions. Despite the loss of most of their lands, the hardships of reservation life, and exposure to the overwhelming American culture, they honor traditions that are thousands of years old. Blending the ways of the larger society with their own traditions, the Shoshone face their ever-changing world with confidence and courage.

With a smile warm enough to light up a landscape, Eva Charley (Western Shoshone), the author's grandmother, looks to her future from Round Mountain, Nevada, in 1929 (left).

An overview today of Wind River Reservation, in Wyoming (right).

Shoshone Activity

Basket and Beadwork Designs

Activity's Purpose

The purpose of this activity is to introduce Indian beading and designs. Shoshone basketry and beadwork are complex and beautiful art. Many colorful designs and images decorate Shoshone clothing, dance regalia, and baskets. Shoshone peoples used many organic and animal products for decoration. Basket makers still use different colored plants and willows to represent important designs, animals, and images in their art. With the arrival of Europeans, beads were introduced, and beading became an important artistic tradition for the Shoshone. Each tiny bead becomes part of a larger, beautiful tapestry. Beading, however, is only possible when one has an image or beautiful pattern to make.

Equipment:

Colored pencils, graph paper, and pictures of Shoshone designs

Sample of Shoshone beadwork

How to design beadwork patterns:

Step 1: Find an example of Shoshone beadwork from the book. Look for one image or pattern that most appeals to you.

Step 2:   From this pattern, select the color or colors you want for your own design. You can try to copy the colors used in the original work, or you can choose colors of your own.

Step 3:   On the graph paper, begin to color in your design. Imagine that each space on the paper is a bead.

Step 4:   After copying the design onto paper, see how it compares to the original.

Conclusion:

With a design made on paper, you could begin to learn how to bead. Beads, however, can be expensive, and beading is difficult. You must use tools to make a loom, buy the right strings and beads, and decide what you want to decorate. For more information, please see *Technique of North American Indian Beadwork* by Monte Smith and Ralph L. Smith. You can also look at the Shoshone Beadwork website at:

http://members.aol.com/beadedweb2/other.html

Another sample of Shoshone beadwork

Western Shoshone Song
(in Honor of the Earth)

"Imaa Hupia"

Tsaan napuni, tai sokopin,

tsaan napuni, tai sokopin,

oyo paam paan kematu

tsaa napuni, tai sokopin.

Tsaan napuni, tai sokopin,

tsaan napuni, tai sokopin,

Soko tontsiyama, paan kematu

tsaan napuni, tai sokopin.

"The Early Morning Song"

How Beautiful is our land,

how beautiful is our land,

forever, beside the water, the water,

how beautiful is our land.

How beautiful is our land,

how beautiful is our land,

Earth, with flowers on it, next to the water

how beautiful is our land.

Shoshone Chronology

Before European Contact	For countless centuries, Shoshone peoples have lived in the Great Basin. They call their homeland Newe Sogobia.
9,000 Years B.P. (before present)	In present-day Nevada, evidence of early Shoshone peoples reveals elaborate woven mats and bags, human remains, as well as a few burial skeletons preserved in wrapped cloths.
9,000–4,500 Years B.P.	Many rivers and water supplies dry up. Early Great Basin peoples adapt to the region's dry environment and changing plant and animal life.
Late 1600s	Spain colonizes New Mexico. The Spanish bring horses and diseases to many western Indians. Having learned to tame and ride escaped horses, Shoshone peoples migrate in larger numbers and travel over much greater distances.
Mid-1700s	Shoshone groups trade and fight with many different Indian neighbors.
1769–1776	Spanish missionaries and soldiers establish forts and missions in California. They link this new colony with the Spanish colony of New Mexico by passing through Shoshone lands.
Early 1800s	Shoshone groups on the Northern Plains encounter American explorers Lewis and Clark on their route west in 1803. A young Shoshone girl, Sacagawea, becomes a guide and interpreter for the explorers.
1847–1850	Shoshone peoples are displaced from their hunting and gathering lands in western Utah and fight several battles with Mormons and other Americans.
1848–1850s	The Oregon Trail crosses through Northern Shoshone homelands, and the Overland and Humboldt trails to California pass through Western Shoshone homelands. Many Shoshone water supplies and food sources are destroyed.

Mid-1850s	Silver discoveries in Nevada bring tens of thousands of miners into Shoshone homelands. The mines destroy many piñon trees and precious water supplies. Numerous Indian peoples are forced to depend on white communities for food and jobs.
1861	Nevada becomes a state, and Shoshone peoples become tied to U.S. Indian agents for supplies and protection from hostile white settlers.
January 1863	After years of bitter tensions, hostile American soldiers and volunteers search for Shoshone bands in southern Idaho and massacre nearly 300 at Bear River.
October 1863	The Treaty of Ruby Valley grants U.S. citizens passage through Shoshone lands and gives the government access to mineral deposits. The treaty also requires the U.S. government to establish reservations, a promise never kept.
1880s–1920s	Shoshone children are sent to boarding schools, and Christian missions are established.
1930s	Under the Indian New Deal, many Shoshone groups change their governments, and many small bands in Nevada receive reservations.
1950s	Following World War II, testing of nuclear weapons begins on Shoshone lands in Nevada.
1950s–1970s	Indian peoples are encouraged to move to cities, and many reservations lose their self-rule.
1960s–1970s	Indian activism leads to changes in U.S. Indian policy. Indian self-determination becomes the key to progress.
1980s–1990s	Western Shoshone leaders call for an end to nuclear testing, a nuclear test ban treaty, and the return of Shoshone lands.

Glossary

Bands Small, loosely affiliated tribes who live in separate family groups.

Boarding schools Schools developed in the late 1800s where Indian children were forcibly sent and educated in order to "Americanize" them.

Bureau of Land Management Part of the U.S. Department of the Interior, the B.L.M. controls nearly 90 percent of Nevada. It is at odds with Shoshones who claim much of that territory as their ancestral homelands.

California Gold Rush The migration West of tens of thousands of Americans to California following the discovery of gold in the 1840s. This proved to be a disaster for the Shoshone.

Colonies Small, urban Indian communities in Nevada, which have similar status to Indian reservations.

Counting coup An act of bravery and skill performed by warriors, usually on horseback, to humiliate their enemies. Warriors touch an enemy with a coup stick, often without causing injury.

Cradleboard Traditional Shoshone child-rearing papoose used to protect and carry babies and infants.

Dawes Act of 1887 Law passed by Congress intended to reduce the land holdings of Indian tribes and give ownership to individuals.

Great Basin The region of the West between the Sierra Mountain and Rocky Mountain chains.

Hide paintings Colorful pictures of Northern and Eastern Shoshone life drawn on the dried and stretched hides of elks and other animals.

Indian New Deal The United States government policy established in the 1930s that slowed decades of assimilation.

Indian Self-Determination A policy of the U.S. government in the 1970s. It recognized the unique political and cultural status of Indian communities.

Newe Western Shoshone form of self-identification that means "the people."

Newe Sogobia Shoshone term for their homelands in the Great Basin. The term also generally refers to "Mother Earth."

Numic Language spoken by most Shoshone peoples in the Great Basin.

Piñon Single-leaf pine of the central Great Basin and Western Shoshone homelands. Piñon nuts have been the most important food supply for Western Shoshone peoples for centuries.

Powwow An Indian cultural gathering and celebration where dancers and singers perform and pay tribute to each other, family members, veterans, and other community leaders.

Relocation Policy developed as part of the Termination policy of the 1950s. It encouraged Indian peoples to move away from reservations and families to cities in exchange for city jobs and job-training programs.

Termination A U.S. government policy of the 1950s that attempted to end the unique legal status of Indian nations within the United States.

Treaties The legal agreements between the government and different Indian nations for resolving wars, land disputes, and other conflicts.

Wickiup Small, portable houses made of brush, grasses, and tree limbs used by Western Shoshone peoples in the Great Basin.

The author, Ned Blackhawk. "My family and friends deserve special thanks. My father appears in this book as a young boy, as do my aunts and uncle. They have all provided inspiration and guidance in various forms and understand the subject matter of this book far better than I ever will. I now know that growing up Indian in Nevada was far more difficult than I can imagine."

Further Reading

Crum, Steven J. *The Road on Which We Came: A History of the Western Shoshone*. Salt Lake City: University of Utah Press, 1994.

Gleiter, Jan, and Kathleen Thompson. *Sacagawea* (First Biographies series). Austin, TX: Raintree Steck-Vaughn, 1995.

Harney, Corbin. *The Way It Is*. Nevada City: Blue Dolphin Publishing, 1995.

Smith, Monte, and Ralph L. Smith. *Technique of North American Indian Beadwork*. Eagle's View Publishing, 1983.

Sources

Bergon, Frank. *Shoshone Mike*. New York: Viking Penguin, 1987.

Hebard, Grace Raymond. *Washakie: Chief of the Shoshones*. Reprint. Lincoln: University of Nebraska Press, 1995.

Hyde, Dayton O. *The Last Free Man: The True Story Behind the Massacre of Shoshone Mike and His Band of Indians in 1911*. New York: The Dial Press, 1973.

Madsen, Brigham D. *The Shoshoni Frontier and the Bear River Massacre*. Salt Lake City: University of Utah Press, 1985.

Smith, Anne M. *Shoshone Tales*. Salt Lake City: University of Utah Press, 1993.

Trenholm, Virginia Cole, and Maurine Carley. *The Shoshonis: Sentinels of the Rockies*. Norman: University of Oklahoma Press, 1964.

Vander, Judith. *Shoshone Ghost Dance Religion: Poetry Songs and Great Basin Context*. Urbana: University of Illinois Press, 1997.

Index

Numbers in italics indicate illustration or map.